# THE CHUMASH

## BY LIZ SONNEBORN

CONSULTANT: JULIE TUMAMAIT-STENSLIE,
CHUMASH ELDER/CULTURE KEEPER,
VENTURA COUNTY, CALIFORNIA

LERNER PUBLICATIONS COMPANY
MINNEAPOLIS

**ABOUT THE COVER IMAGE:** This is a traditional Chumash basket. Chumash baskets are famous throughout the world.

PHOTO ACKNOWLEDGMENTS:

The photos in this book are used courtesy of: Courtesy of the Southwest Museum, Los Angeles, Photo # (N.37022), p. 5; © Marilyn "Angel" Wynn/Nativestock.com, pp. 7, 8, 10, 14, 15, 17, 18, 21, 23, 26, 45; © Steve Terrill/CORBIS, p. 13; Courtesy of the Bancroft Library, University of California Berkeley, pp. 16, 42; © Ray Bial, pp. 19, 20, 24, 28, 46, 47, 48; Agricultural Research Service, USDA, p. 25; Courtesy of the Ventura County Museum of History & Art, p. 30; © Chuck Place/ PlaceStockPhoto.com, p. 31; Collection of the Santa Barbara Historical Society, p. 33; © North Wind Picture Archives, p. 34; Library of Congress, pp. 35 (LC-USZ62-38775), 41(LC-USZ62-740), 44 (LC-USZ62-108463); Illustration by John Graham, p. 43; Robert V. Schwemmer, NOAA, Channel Islands National Marine Sanctuary, Santa Barbara, CA, p. 50.

Front Cover: Len Wood's Indian Territory Gallery, Laguna Beach, CA.

Lerner Publications Company
A division of Lerner Publishing Group
241 First Avenue North
Minneapolis, MN 55401 U.S.A.

Website address: www.lernerbooks.com


Library of Congress Cataloging-in-Publication Data

Sonneborn, Liz.
    The Chumash / by Liz Sonneborn.
      p.    cm. — (Native American histories)
    Includes bibliographical references and index.
    ISBN-13: 978-0-8225-5912-2 (lib. bdg. : alk. paper)
    ISBN-10: 0-8225-5912-9 (lib. bdg. : alk. paper)
    1. Chumash Indians—History. 2. Chumash Indians—Social life and customs. 3. Chumash Indians—Religion. I. Title. II. Series.
    E99.C815S68 2007
    979.4004'9758-dc22                                              2005024009

Manufactured in the United States of America
1 2 3 4 5 6 – BP – 12 11 10 09 08 07

# CONTENTS

# CHAPTER 1

# A LAND OF PLENTY

**THE CHUMASH ARE NATIVE AMERICANS.** Native North Americans are also called American Indians. The Chumash have lived in North America for thousands of years. They made their home in present-day California.

The early Chumash lived in many villages. These villages covered about seven thousand square miles. Some Chumash lived inland. Others lived on the coast of the Pacific Ocean. Still others lived on the Channel Islands off the coast of California. These islands include Santa Cruz, Santa Rosa, and Anacapa.

The Chumash's homeland was rich in natural resources. It provided the Chumash with every necessity. American Indians in many other places had to struggle to survive. But with just a little effort, the Chumash could find everything they needed to live. Food was especially plentiful.

The early Chumash used California's rich natural resources to make good lives for themselves.

# CREATION OF THE CHUMASH

The Chumash tell many different stories to explain their people's origins. One story says that Hutash, the Earth Goddess, gathered the seeds of a magic plant. From the seeds, she made the first Chumash Indians. They lived on Santa Cruz Island.

Hutash's husband, Sky Snake, shot lightning bolts at the humans. This gave them fire. With fire to warm them, the Chumash lived well. Their villages grew. Soon the island was crowded.

The Chumash made so much noise that Hutash could not sleep. To solve the problem, she made a rainbow. It stretched from the island to the mainland. Many Chumash walked across the rainbow bridge. Some looked down. They became dizzy and fell into the water. Hutash turned them into dolphins. But most made it to the mainland and built new villages there.

Chumash men caught fish. They made fishing hooks and spears from bones and shells. They also wove fishing nets from plant materials.

Coastal fishers collected mussels and clams on the beach. If they were lucky, a whale might wash up onshore. Then everyone in the village would feast on whale meat. The Chumash used every part of the whale. They even used the bones.

Chumash men were also hunters. They stalked deer, bears, and mountain lions. Sometimes hunters dressed up like animals so they could sneak up on their prey. They often wore antlers and deerskins. The Chumash also hunted small animals. These included rabbits, squirrels, and grasshoppers.

This Chumash hunter is dressed as a wolf. He is using a shoulder sling to throw a hunting spear.

Women gathered wild plants to eat. In baskets, they collected nuts, seeds, roots, and bulbs. The most important food for the Chumash were acorns. Acorns contain a bitter-tasting substance called tannin. To remove the tannin, the women ground up the nuts and mixed them with water. The water washed the tannin out. Next, the women cooked the acorn meal. This made a tasty and filling mush. The Chumash ate acorn mush at nearly every meal.

Chumash women prepare acorn mush.

## A TRIBE OF TRADERS

Chumash villages traded with one another. As a result, the Chumash always had a variety of foods to eat. Villagers on an island would trade their fish for meat and acorns from a mainland village.

The Chumash also traded with other American Indians. On land, Chumash traders traveled along foot trails. Some modern highways follow the paths of these old trails. Traders also traveled by water in large wooden canoes called *tomols*. A long tomol could hold as many as ten people.

## THE BROTHERHOOD OF THE TOMOL

The best Chumash seafarers belonged to a special organization. It was called the Brotherhood of the Tomol. Not everyone could join. A man had to apply and pay a fee. The brotherhood taught new members their secrets for making tomols. Being a member of the group was a great honor. The brotherhood included some of the richest and most respected people in Chumash society.

The Chumash often built tomols out of redwood.

Only the most skilled craftspeople could make tomols. They usually built the boats out of redwood. Redwood trees did not grow in Chumash territory. But pieces of redwood often washed up on the beach. If a tomol maker didn't have redwood, he used pine instead.

Using stone and bone tools, a tomol maker split wood into flat pieces called planks. After smoothing the wood, he glued the planks together with tar.

The tomol maker then drilled holes in the planks and tied them together. He used rope made from milkweed plants. Next, the tomol maker spread tar over the wood. This made it waterproof. As a final step, he decorated the tomol with red paint and pieces of shell.

The Chumash were grateful to tomol makers. Their beautiful boats allowed the Chumash to visit friends in other villages. Because of the tomols, the Chumash remained a close-knit people.

# CHAPTER 2
# LIFE IN A CHUMASH VILLAGE

## TRADITIONALLY, THE CHUMASH LIVED IN HUNDREDS OF VILLAGES.

Some were just small clusters of homes. But the largest looked like towns. Most large villages were on the coast. Chumash from other areas regularly visited the coastal villages to trade.

The Chumash built all of their villages near water. Inland villages were often near rivers. Chumash villages were also close to good areas for hunting and gathering wild plants. One plant that grew in marshy areas was especially important to the Chumash. This was the tule, or bulrush.

Tule grows in lakes, marshes, and other wetlands.

## LIVING TOGETHER

The Chumash used tule stalks to cover their houses. To make a house, the Chumash first built a dome-shaped frame. It was made from bent willow poles. Onto the frame, they tied tule in chunks. The chunks looked like shingles. Builders left a hole at the top of the house. The hole let smoke escape if they built a fire inside. When it rained, the Chumash covered the smoke hole with a tule flap.

Chunks of tule cover this traditional Chumash home.

Inside a Chumash house were tule mats. The Chumash used the mats as seating areas. The Chumash also put mats on top of raised platforms. People slept on these platforms. They used the spaces below the platforms for storage. In the winter, a tule mat covered the doorway to keep out the cold.

In each house lived a family of parents, children, and usually grandparents or other relatives. The Chumash arranged their houses in neat rows. They left small paths between the rows. They used these paths to walk around the village.

Chumash grandparents often lived with their adult children. The grandparents helped educate their grandchildren.

Each village had a storehouse. It was full of acorns and other foods. Sometimes village leaders offered the stored food to visitors. At other times, they gave it to the poor. There was also at least one sweat lodge. Inside, the Chumash sat around a fire. The steam from the fire caused them to sweat. They believed that sweating cleansed their bodies. After leaving a sweat lodge, the Chumash often jumped into nearby rivers or lakes to cool off.

American Indians plunge into a cool river after sitting in a steamy sweat lodge *(far right)*.

Villagers often built sun shelters such as this one. The shelters provided shady places for craftspeople to work.

Villages also had areas set aside for special activities. There was a playground, where children could gather to play games. There was also a dancing ground, where the Chumash held religious ceremonies.

## CRAFTING GOODS

In Chumash villages, craftspeople had special spaces to do their work. Using tule, skins, stones, shells, and wood, craftspeople made just about everything the Chumash needed.

A display of traditional Chumash clothing and jewelry

Clothing was one of the easiest things to make, because the Chumash wore very little. In warm weather, a woman wore only a skirt. A man usually wore nothing at all. When it was colder, the Chumash sometimes wrapped themselves in animal furs.

The Chumash liked to adorn themselves with paint and jewelry. People from each village painted their bodies with distinctive designs. Women wore necklaces and earrings. Men sometimes wore pieces of cane in holes in their earlobes. They also tied strings of bone, wood, and stone ornaments in their long hair.

The Chumash used stones to make tools, knives, and arrowheads. They traded with other American Indians to get a soft stone called steatite. Chumash craftspeople used steatite to make cooking pots. Craftspeople also carved bowls and plates out of wood.

The Chumash used many handmade tools, such as this arrowhead.

## MAKING MONEY

The name *Chumash* comes from the word *michumash*. *Michumash* was the Chumash name for the people who lived on Santa Cruz Island. The name means "bead money makers." The Santa Cruz Chumash made their own money out of olivella shells. They broke the shells into pieces. They then drilled holes into the pieces to make

beads *(left)*. They used the beads as money. The Chumash used bead money to buy things such as tools, nets, leather, meat, acorns, and plants for medicine.

The Chumash were great basket weavers. They made different types of baskets for gathering, storing, preparing, and serving food. Sometimes they covered the inside of a basket with tar. The basket could then hold water without leaking. Craftspeople also made special baskets to hold shell money or other valuables.

The Chumash wove baskets from plant stalks. They decorated the baskets with simple but elegant designs. A typical Chumash basket was tan. It had a dark band near the top. Sometimes a basket had many dark stripes or zigzags on it. The Chumash are known throughout the world for their baskets. Some believe they are the most beautiful made by any American Indian tribe.

Chumash baskets such as these are both beautiful and useful.

# CHAPTER 3

# LEADING THE PEOPLE

**IN EACH CHUMASH VILLAGE, ONE HOUSE WAS BIGGER THAN THE REST.** It belonged to the *wot*. The wot was the village's leader. Usually, a wot inherited his position. Both men and women could be wots. But most were men.

The wot's main responsibility was to care for the poor and elderly. The Chumash thought that it was wrong for anyone to go hungry. The wot kept extra food to give to people in need.

In larger villages, the wot had other duties. He might assign people to different hunting and gathering areas. Or he might collect supplies for religious ceremonies and social gatherings.

Once in a while, villages had disputes with one another. For example, they might both claim the same fishing area. Sometimes the warriors of two villages fought one another. But often, the two wots came together to talk about the problem. They tried to work out a peaceful solution.

Fish were an important part of the Chumash diet. Sometimes two villages claimed the same fishing area. Their wots might meet to solve the problem fairly.

## HELPING THE WOT

The wot had help with his duties. Messengers called *ksen* made announcements for the wot. They reported to him about everything going on in the village. The wot also had a group of advisers. They were called the *antap*. The antap were members of a religious society. They were very important people. As children, they learned secret songs and dances that only the antap could know.

Cave paintings such as this one might have had religious importance for the Chumash.

Chumash shamans asked patients to swallow live red ants.
Many Chumash believed the ants could help them get well.

Some members of the antap were shamans.
Shamans interpreted dreams and healed the sick.
The shamans used songs and prayers to cure
people. Sometimes shamans encouraged patients
to swallow live red ants. They believed the ants
would make their patients well. They also made
medicines out of plants. For instance, the shamans
gave patients a carrotlike root to chew. They
believed the root helped fight disease.

This is a cave painting of a swordfish. Traditionally, the Chumash sometimes asked a swordfish spirit for food. They believed that the swordfish spirit could send a whale to shore.

The Chumash believed a spiritual power was at work in the universe. The shamans helped people feel connected to this special power. They also showed each person how to find a spirit helper. Spirit helpers watched out for people and kept them safe. Spirit helpers also gave people power. A helper might be a plant, an animal, or a relative who had died.

When people had a vision of a spirit helper, they would carve an image of it. They kept the carving with them at all times. If they lost the charm, they feared something awful might happen.

## THE THREE WORLDS

The Chumash believed there were three worlds. The worlds were like flat, round trays with spaces between them. Giant serpents held up the Middle World. The Middle World was an island with water all around it. An eagle held up the Upper World. The Upper World was home to powerful beings, including the Sun, the Moon, and the North Star. The Lower World was a scary place. Frightening creatures called Nunasis lived there. Sometimes, at night, the Nunasis left their world. They came up to the Middle World and scared anyone who saw them.

The antap also included people called *paxa*. Paxa supervised the performance of ceremonies. The Chumash believed these ceremonies kept their world in balance.

## CEREMONIAL LIFE

One ceremony honored the goddess Hutash. It was a thanksgiving ceremony. The ceremony took place late in the summer to celebrate the acorn harvest. During this happy time, people prayed, feasted, sang, danced, and played games.

## FUN AND GAMES

At any gathering, the Chumash loved to play games. Children played kickball, marbles, and shinny. Shinny is a team sport similar to hockey. Players use a stick and a wooden ball *(shown at right)*. Sometimes more than two hundred players could be on the field.

In the winter, the Chumash gathered for the Winter Solstice Ceremony. It took place in December, on the shortest day of the year. During the ceremony, thirteen paxa set up a sunstick. A sunstick was a stone disk set on top of a pole. When the sun hit the disk, it cast a huge shadow. This ceremony celebrated the sun's power. The Chumash believed that the ceremony helped bring sunny days in the spring.

Traditionally, paxa supervised ceremonies such as this one.

Ceremonies often lasted for days. People gathered in their villages' dance grounds to watch the festivities. Musicians played whistles and flutes. Dancers performed, wearing special clothing.

The Chumash man *(standing, right)* is wearing special jewelry, body paint, and a feathered headdress. He is dancing in a Chumash ceremony at the 1936 Ventura County fair in California.

This display includes a variety of Chumash flutes and rattles. The Chumash used these instruments in ceremonies.

One part of the Hutash ceremony was the Bear Dance. In the Bear Dance, one dancer wore a feathered headdress. He also had two bear paws around his neck. The bear dancer was allowed to bite anyone who made too much noise during his dance.

Many ceremonies were also social occasions. They allowed people from various villages to spend time with one another. Together they sang songs, played games, and told stories. At these gatherings, the Chumash not only celebrated the spirit world. They also enjoyed the company of friends and relatives.

# CHAPTER 4

# THE SPANISH ARRIVE

**IN 1542, TWO GREAT SHIPS APPEARED OFF THE COAST OF CHUMASH TERRITORY.** The ships were from Spain. Portuguese explorer Juan Rodríguez Cabrillo commanded the ships. Cabrillo and his crew were the first Europeans to meet the Chumash.

The Chumash came out to greet the strangers. Many climbed into tomols and paddled toward the ships. One of the Spaniards wrote about the encounter. He reported that "the Indians were very friendly. . . . [A]ll the way there were many canoes . . . and many Indians kept boarding the ships."

For the next two hundred years, other Spanish ships sometimes sailed into Chumash waters. But the Spaniards never stayed long.

In 1542, the Chumash paddled their tomols out to meet the Spaniards' large ships.

American Indians of California first met Catholic priests in the late 1700s.

The situation changed in 1769. That year, a group of Spanish men arrived in the Chumash homeland. Gaspar de Portolá led the men. Portolá did not just want to visit the Chumash. He wanted to build permanent Spanish settlements among them.

## SETTLING IN

Two Catholic priests came with Portolá. Between 1772 and 1804, the priests built five missions in Chumash territory. A mission was a group of buildings. It included a church and housing. At the missions, the priests worked to teach the Chumash about Christianity.

The Spanish brought the Chumash new ideas and new goods. These included metal tools and horses. But the Spanish also made the Chumash work at the missions. And the Spanish introduced new diseases to the tribe. The Chumash had never been exposed to diseases such as measles and smallpox. As a result, thousands of Chumash who caught these illnesses died. This time was hard for the Chumash. The survivors were very sad.

The Spanish brought horses to North America.

Worshippers leave a service at Mission Santa Barbara in the 1800s. The Spanish founded the mission in 1786.

## THE MISSION ERA

Life at the missions was often hard. The Chumash had to work many hours a day. The priests made the Chumash give up their old ways. They had to become Christians.

The Chumash also had to live as the Spaniards did. The priests taught them to farm and raise animals. These ways of getting food were much more work than hunting, fishing, and gathering plants.

Plowing land to plant a crop was hard work.

Until 1810, the Spanish government had sent money and supplies to the missions. But then, Mexico rebelled against Spain. Spain gave Mexico its independence in 1821. This left Mexico in charge of the missions.

Mexico had little money to spend on the missions. It shut them down in 1834. Mexico gave the missions' land to a few Spanish families. It was their reward for supporting the Mexican government.

**PACOMIO** was born in a Chumash village. He came to live at the mission at La Purísima when he was a boy. As he grew older, Pacomio became angry at the way the Mexicans treated the American Indians there. Pacomio secretly formed an army to drive the Mexicans from California. In 1824, he led an attack at La Purísima. The Mexicans fought back. Eventually, they regained control of the mission. The Mexicans then sent Pacomio away to live at Monterey. The citizens of that Mexican town liked him so much they elected him mayor.

The Mexican government gave La Purísima *(above)* to a Spanish family. They used the priests' housing for a stable.

Suddenly, the Chumash were homeless and landless. Some took jobs with the families that controlled their old lands. These Chumash worked as cowboys and servants. Others moved inland. They joined other American Indian groups. These included the Yokuts and the Kitanemuk.

Wherever they went, the Chumash lost their old way of life. Poor and desperate, their population fell. Before the Spanish came, there were about 20,000 Chumash Indians. By 1840, only about 250 Chumash were left.

# CHAPTER 5

# THE MODERN CHUMASH

**IN 1848, THE CHUMASH MET ANOTHER GROUP OF PEOPLE.** They were from the United States. They called themselves Americans. The United States had just won a war with Mexico. As part of the peace treaty, or agreement, the Americans took control of California.

Within months, many Americans were rushing into the area. Gold had been discovered in northern California. Americans came there with dreams of striking it rich. When they found no gold, many people moved into the Chumash's old territory. The newcomers built farms and ranches there.

Starting in 1848, many white Americans rushed to California to dig for gold.

## AMONG AMERICANS

Americans often treated California Indians badly. They called them savages and drove them from their homes. A California law let Californians force American Indians to work for them. Because of this law, some Chumash lived like slaves.

To protect themselves, the Chumash tried to hide their true culture. Many began speaking English or Spanish. Some even changed their names. Soon there were very few people who knew the Chumash language.

The U.S. government forced many groups of American Indians to leave their homes and live on reservations.

**FERNANDO LIBRADO,** also known as Kitsepawit, was born at a Spanish mission in 1839. He spent much of his life traveling while looking for work on ranches. Wherever he went, he sought out other Chumash. Librado always asked them about old Chumash customs, songs, and stories. In 1912, John P. Harrington began meeting with Librado. Harrington was an anthropologist. Anthropologists study how people lived in the past. Librado told Harrington everything he knew about the Chumash. Librado also built a tomol for Harrington. He was the only Chumash who remembered how to make one. Librado's work with Harrington helped preserve information about the tribe's old ways.

The surviving Chumash scattered. Some moved to cities such as Santa Barbara and Ventura. Others lived on ranches. There they worked as laborers or maids. But a few Chumash families still lived together near the old Santa Ynez mission.

In the 1800s, many Chumash lived on ranches and farms. This Native American home and orchard was near U.S. Fort Tejon in Kern County, California. Inland Chumash villages had been in the area before the fort was built.

A Chumash couple from the late 1800s pose for a photograph in the garden of a former California mission.

In 1901, the U.S. government set aside seventy-five acres of land for the Chumash. The area is known as the Santa Ynez Reservation. The people there are called the Santa Ynez Band of Chumash Indians.

For decades, the Chumash at Santa Ynez were very poor. Many had to work several jobs just to get by. Some of their houses did not have electricity or running water.

Conditions at Santa Ynez began to improve in the 1960s and 1970s. In 1968, the Chumash there drafted a constitution. The constitution explains how the Chumash government works. They also formed a five-member business committee. Its members tried to bring businesses to the reservation. In 1976, the Santa Ynez Chumash opened a tribal hall.

The next year, the U.S. government began giving Santa Ynez funds to build better houses. Chumash from other areas started moving to Santa Ynez.

The Chumash tribal office at the Santa Ynez Reservation

In modern times, new houses are common on the Santa Ynez Reservation.

## NEW WAYS, OLD TRADITIONS

The Chumash's fortunes improved even more in 2000. That year, California voters decided to let the Santa Ynez Chumash build a casino. At casinos, people play games and try to win money. Two years later, the Santa Ynez Band opened the Chumash Casino Resort.

The Chumash Casino Resort attracts thousands of visitors each year. The resort includes a fancy hotel and many restaurants.

The business committee has used the income from the resort to help the Santa Ynez Chumash. Reservation residents enjoy a new health clinic. They also have a new community center and computer lab.

The Chumash Casino Resort is located in Santa Ynez, California, about 125 miles north of Los Angeles.

**VINCENT ARMENTA** moved to the Santa Ynez Reservation as a teenager in 1979. After graduating from high school, he earned a living as a welder. Armenta became involved in tribal politics. In 1999, he won the election for tribal chairman of the Santa Ynez Band. He worked hard to develop the Chumash Casino Resort. This business has earned a great deal of money for his people. The Santa Ynez Chumash have reelected him twice.

The Santa Ynez Band is the only official Chumash tribe. It has about 150 members. But there are about 3,500 other Chumash in the United States. Many still live in California. Some are trying to persuade the United States to make them members of an official tribe as well.

The Chumash are also working hard to revive their old traditions. Some young people are studying the Chumash language. Others are learning how to weave baskets. Still others are fighting to protect places that have religious importance to the Chumash.

The Chumash also remain proud seafarers. In recent years, some have worked with boatbuilders to help build tomols. These beautiful canoes have always helped unite the Chumash. In September 2005, a group of young men paddled a tomol from the California coast to Santa Cruz Island. A crowd of about two hundred people gathered on the island. They cheered and sang when they saw the boat. Their voices celebrated the past and present of the great Chumash people.

A crew paddled a special tomol to Santa Cruz Island in September 2005. Its name is *?Elye?wun*, or "Swordfish," in Chumash.

# CHUMASH CAVE PAINTING

The Chumash painted the walls of caves with beautiful, colorful designs. Their favorite colors included black, red, orange, yellow, and white. Shamans probably made most of the paintings. They believed that the paintings would influence the spirit beings. With store-bought paints and a rock you find outside, you can create your own version of a Chumash cave painting.

## WHAT YOU NEED:

*acrylic paints in black, red, orange, yellow, and white*
*one or two paintbrushes*
*a rock with a fairly flat surface, about 6 × 6 inches or larger*

## WHAT TO DO:

1. Study the photographs of Chumash cave paintings on pages 24 and 26. Notice the colors and shapes the Chumash painters used.
2. Use your paints to create similar designs on the flattest side of the rock you've chosen.

# PLACES TO VISIT

**Chumash Painted Cave State Historic Park**
*Santa Barbara County, California*
(805) 733-3713
http://www.parks.ca.gov/default.asp?page_id=602
At the center of this small park north of Santa Barbara is a cave painted by the Chumash. The cave painting is about two hundred years old.

**Mission Santa Barbara**
*Santa Barbara, California*
(805) 682-4149
http://www.sbmission.org/history.shtml
Founded in 1786, Mission Santa Barbara was one of five missions in Chumash territory. Visitors can tour its buildings, which offer a beautiful view of the city of Santa Barbara.

**Oakbrook Regional Park Chumash Interpretive Center**
*Thousand Oaks, California*
(805) 492-8076
http://www.designplace.com/chumash
This cultural center features Chumash paintings and artifacts. It also offers guided tours and educational programs for visitors.

**Santa Barbara Museum of Natural History**
*Santa Barbara, California*
(805) 682-4711
http://www.sbnature.org
This museum has one of the largest collections of Chumash objects in the world. On display are baskets, pots, tools, and musical instruments. There is also a plank canoe built in 1913.

# GLOSSARY

**antap:** members of an important religious society that advised a Chumash village leader

**anthropologist:** a scientist who studies the way people lived in the past

**ksen:** messengers who made announcements for and reported to a Chumash village leader

**mission:** a group of buildings in which people of a certain religion work to teach others about their beliefs

**paxa:** people who supervised the performance of Chumash ceremonies

**reservation:** an area of land set aside by the U.S. government for use by a particular American Indian group

**shaman:** an American Indian healer

**sweat lodge:** a heated structure in which people cleanse their bodies by sweating

**tomol:** a Chumash canoe

**treaty:** an agreement between two or more nations

**tribe:** a group of related American Indians who share the same language, customs, and religious beliefs

**wot:** the leader of a Chumash village

# FURTHER READING

Behrens, June. *Missions of the Central Coast*. Minneapolis: Lerner
Publishing Group, 1996. With color pictures throughout, this book
describes the lives of Chumash Indians at four California missions.

Bial, Raymond. *The Chumash*. New York: Benchmark Books, 2004. This
title explores the traditional world of the Chumash.

Dengler, Marianna. *The Worry Stone*. Flagstaff, AZ: Rising Moon, 1996.
An elderly woman befriends a lonely boy and tells him the tales of
the worry stone. This special rock's story is interwoven with that of
the Chumash people.

Nelson, Libby. *California Missions: Projects & Layouts*. With Kari A.
Cornell. Minneapolis: Lerner Publishing Group, 1997. This title
about the California missions offers easy-to-follow instructions on
building your own model of a California mission.

Schwabacher, Martin. *The Chumash Indians*. New York: Chelsea House
Publishers, 1995. This book includes discussions of Chumash history,
culture, and religious beliefs.

Van Steenwyk, Elizabeth. *The California Missions*. New York: Franklin
Watts, 1995. This title provides a useful introduction to California's
mission period.

Young, Robert. *A Personal Tour of La Purísima*. Minneapolis: Lerner
Publishing Group, 1999. This source looks at how two Chumash
Indians, two Spanish soldiers, and one priest lived at La Purísima
mission.

# WEBSITES

**Chumash Indian Life, Santa Barbara Museum of Natural History**
http://www.sbnature.org/research/anthro/chumash/index.htm
This site features information on Chumash life and history based on
objects in the museum's collection.

**Santa Ynez Band of Chumash Indians**
http://www.santaynezchumash.org
This page includes cultural and historical information on the Santa
Ynez Band of Chumash.

# SELECTED BIBLIOGRAPHY

Gibson, Robert O. *The Chumash*. New York: Chelsea House Publishers,
1991.

Hoxie, Frederick E., ed. *Encyclopedia of North American Indians*. Boston:
Houghton Mifflin, 1996.

McCall, Lynne, and Rosalind Perry, proj. coords. *The Chumash People:
Materials for Teachers and Students*. Rev. ed. San Luis Obispo, CA.: EZ
Nature Books, 1991.

Miller, Bruce W. *Chumash: A Picture of Their World*. Los Osos, CA: Sand
River Press, 1988.

# INDEX